THE
Mysterious Rays

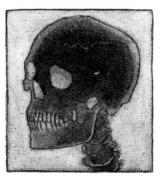

OF DR. RÖNTGEN

THE
Mysterious Rays
OF DR. RÖNTGEN

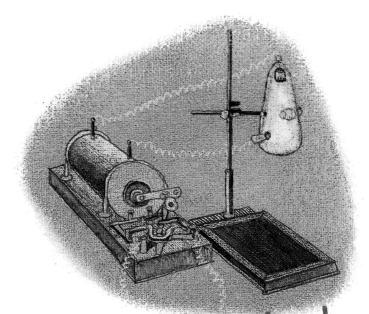

BY
BEVERLY GHERMAN

ILLUSTRATED BY
STEPHEN MARCHESI

ATHENEUM   1994   NEW YORK

Maxwell Macmillan Canada
Toronto
Maxwell Macmillan International
New York   Oxford   Singapore   Sydney

With gratitude to Dr. Jim Haag, physics professor and friend,
for his careful reading of the manuscript

Atheneum
Macmillan Publishing Company
866 Third Avenue
New York, NY 10022

Maxwell Macmillan Canada, Inc.
1200 Eglinton Avenue East
Suite 200
Don Mills, Ontario M3C 3N1

Macmillan Publishing Company is part of
the Maxwell Communication Group of Companies.

First edition

Printed in Singapore on recycled paper
10 9 8 7 6 5 4 3 2 1

The text of this book is set in Sabon.

The illustrations are rendered in oil paints.

Library of Congress Cataloging-in-Publication Data

Gherman, Beverly.
The mysterious rays of Dr. Röntgen / by Beverly Gherman;
illustrated by Stephen Marchesi.
p.   cm.
Includes bibliographical references.
Summary: Describes the work of Wilhelm Röntgen, the
German physicist who won the first Nobel Prize in Physics
in 1901 for his discovery of X rays.
ISBN 0–689–31839–1
1. Röntgen, Wilhelm Conrad, 1845–1923—Juvenile
literature. 2. X rays—Juvenile literature. 3 Physicists—
Germany—Biography—Juvenile literature. [1. Röntgen,
Wilhelm Conrad, 1845–1923. 2. Physicists. 3. X rays.]
I. Marchesi, Stephen, ill. II. Title.
QC16.R487G43   1994
539.7′222′092—dc20
[B]   92–38966

For Alan and Janet, who sparked the idea,
and for Dotty, who brought it closer to home
—B. G.

For my brothers Louis and Dennis
—S. M.

TABLE OF CONTENTS

CHAPTER ONE

ALONE IN THE LABORATORY

Every night Professor Wilhelm Röntgen worked late in his laboratory in Würzburg, Germany, testing electricity and measuring magnetic effects. Often he forgot to go upstairs for supper.

One November night in 1895 his wife Bertha sent their servant downstairs to the laboratory to remind her husband that supper was ready. Still he did not come.

Again Bertha sent the servant and again she waited for Wilhelm to come upstairs.

At last he appeared, his thick black hair on end, his bushy beard askew. He sat at the table, ate a few bites, checked the time on his gold watch, and then rushed back to the laboratory.

For the next few weeks Wilhelm stayed in his laboratory night and day. He ate there. He slept there. But mainly he worked there, repeating his experiments.

No one knew what he was investigating behind closed doors. Bertha had no idea. His students had no clue. The other professors had no inkling what Wilhelm was studying.

"I have discovered something interesting" was all he would say.

CHAPTER TWO

A NEW KIND OF RAY

Finally Wilhelm brought Bertha down to the laboratory. He placed her hand on a photographic plate used to take pictures and told her not to move. He wanted to take a picture of her hand. Then he pulled the drapes and put out the lamps. It was pitch black in the laboratory.

Wilhelm turned on a switch that sent electricity through his equipment. The only sound in the laboratory was the ticking of the clock. Five minutes passed. Ten minutes. After fifteen minutes Wilhelm lifted Bertha's hand.

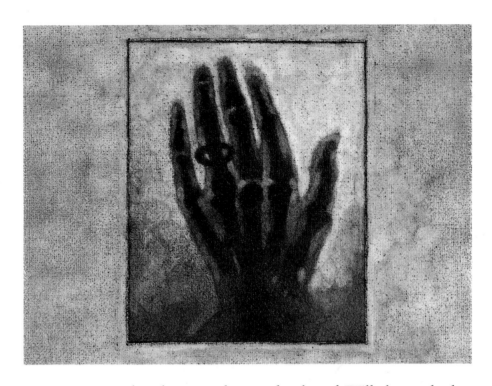

As soon as the photograph was developed Wilhelm rushed to show it to Bertha. She looked at it and shuddered with fear. She saw a picture of bones—her bones—and they made her think of skeletons and death. Her wedding ring seemed to be floating around a bony finger.

Wilhelm tried to comfort Bertha, telling her not to be afraid. "I have discovered invisible rays," he said. These rays penetrate living flesh and show our bones. They also let us see through boxes and books, he explained.

Wilhelm called them X rays because X stood for the unknown. Although he didn't know what they were, he knew they were important. "This is something new," he told Bertha. "I must investigate."

He built himself a tin box large enough to work in. From inside the darkened box Wilhelm continued to study the rays. He realized that just as sunlight passed through a glass window, the new rays passed through wood or flesh or other nonmetallic objects.

CHAPTER THREE

THE DISCOVERY EXPLAINED

By January, Wilhelm was ready to explain his discovery at a scientific meeting. Softly, almost shyly, he said he had heard about studies others were doing with airtight glass tubes known as Crookes tubes. He wanted to repeat their studies and carry out some of his own using these vacuum tubes.

He described how he had set up his equipment on that November night. First he covered a Crookes vacuum tube with black paper so that no light could escape from it. Then he connected the tube to electricity. Next he pulled the heavy drapes and turned off all the lamps.

When the laboratory was in total darkness Wilhelm sent electricity through the Crookes tube. He was startled to see a green glow across the darkened room. What caused that glow? he asked himself. He turned off the electricity and the glow disappeared. It could not have come from the Crookes tube, he reasoned, because the tube was completely covered.

Again he turned on the electricity and again he saw the glow. Lighting a match, he noticed that the glow was coming from a paper lying on a bench across the room. The paper was covered with special chemicals, but it did not glow by itself. There had to be some kind of energy causing the chemicals in the paper to glow like that. But what could it be?

Wilhelm moved the chemically treated paper farther away from the Crookes tube. Still it glowed when he turned on the current. He placed a book between the tube and the paper. The glow persisted.

What would block the glow? he wondered. He tried fabric, a wooden box, and finally his own hand. The rays passed through almost everything, he told the hushed group. He then decided to take a picture of his hand. A photograph would give him visual proof that the rays existed.

Would someone in the audience volunteer to have a picture made of his hand? A famous professor came to the stage. Wilhelm placed his hand on a photographic plate just as he had done with Bertha. After many long minutes the photograph was ready. Wilhelm held it up and passed it slowly before the astounded audience. They saw the bones in the professor's hand, joint by joint. It was miraculous! Everyone burst into cheers and insisted the rays be named Röntgen rays after Wilhelm.

His friends told him to take out a patent on his discovery. He would become rich as well as famous, they said. As a scientist Wilhelm wanted to share his knowledge with others and help find positive uses for X rays. He felt his discovery belonged to the world, and he did not care about patents and making money.

CHAPTER FOUR

NEWS TRAVELS

The news traveled across Europe and over the ocean to the United States. Almost overnight Wilhelm became famous and began to receive more mail than he could answer.

Reporters came to interview him.

"Is it light?" one asked.

"No," he said.

"Is it electricity?"

"Not in any known form," he replied.

"What is it?"

"I don't know," Wilhelm answered in all honesty.

In a letter to Wilhelm's cousin, Bertha wrote that since the discovery their life was no longer the same. "Often we are almost dizzy with all the praise and honors," she admitted.

Scientists all around the world began studying X rays. That first year there were at least a thousand papers published describing those studies.

Doctors found immediate uses for X rays. Now they could locate bullets or broken bones in their patients' bodies. They could even see where Siamese twins were joined.

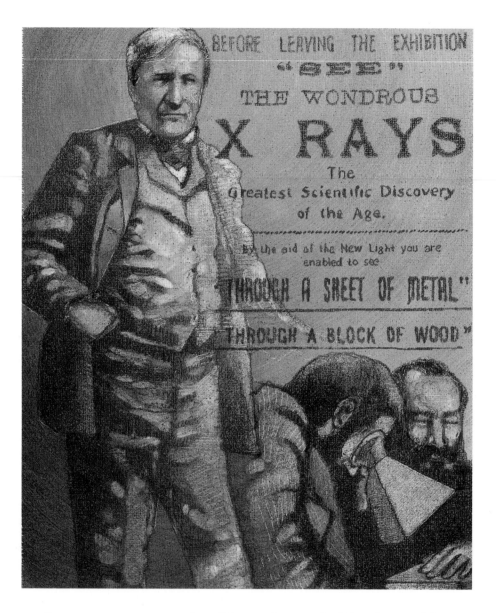

Soon everyone wanted an X-ray picture. In New Jersey, Thomas Edison, the inventor of the electric light, began experimenting with X rays. Instead of taking permanent photographs, he used a fluorescent screen similar to a movie screen and people lined up for the novelty of seeing their bones displayed right through their clothing.

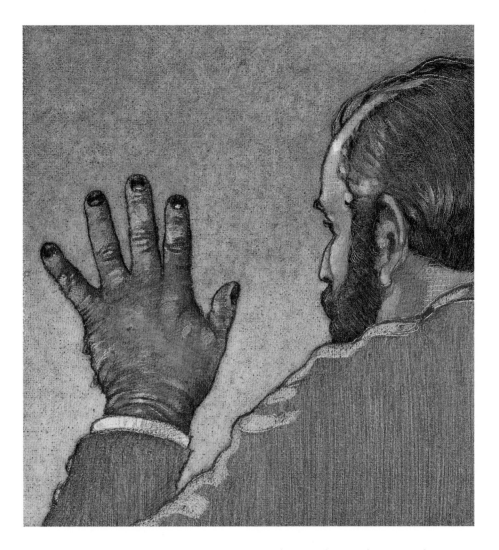

Then something terrible happened. People working with X rays began to get sick. Mr. Hawks, who demonstrated a machine in Bloomingdale Brothers Department Store, noticed the skin from his hands turning red and peeling off. His fingernails stopped growing. His hair began falling out.

Edison's assistant, Clarence Dally, had to have his left hand amputated when its skin rotted away. He also lost several fingers on his right hand. Six years later he died. There were many others who suffered and died from overexposure to X rays.

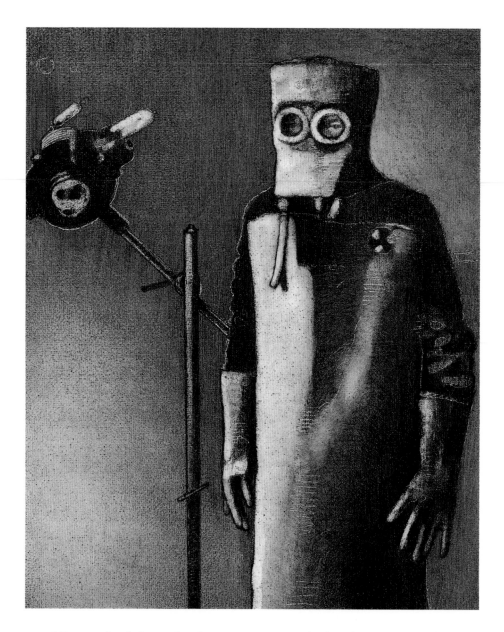

No one had thought the new rays might be dangerous. Without realizing its importance, Wilhelm had used a lead lining in his tin box, which had protected him against the rays. Soon everyone would use lead for protection. They would also learn to lower the exposure time and reduce the amount of rays used.

In 1901 the first Nobel Prize in physics was awarded to Wilhelm for his discovery of X rays. He traveled to Stockholm, Sweden, for the ceremony, but in his will he gave the prize money to the University of Würzburg for research. As honored as he was to receive the prize, Wilhelm told Bertha, his greatest personal reward came from having solved a problem through careful research.

How pleased Wilhelm would be to know the many advances made with X rays since his discovery. Today art experts study paintings with them to be sure the paintings are not fakes. Engineers use them to be certain that machinery and equipment are properly made. Airport workers scan baggage in search of bombs, weapons, and drugs.

With X rays, doctors have learned to study every part of the body and use the rays to treat many forms of cancer. Dentists find cavities or disease in teeth and bones. Scientists study fossils to learn how ancient animals looked and lived. They also study the bones and teeth of mummies.

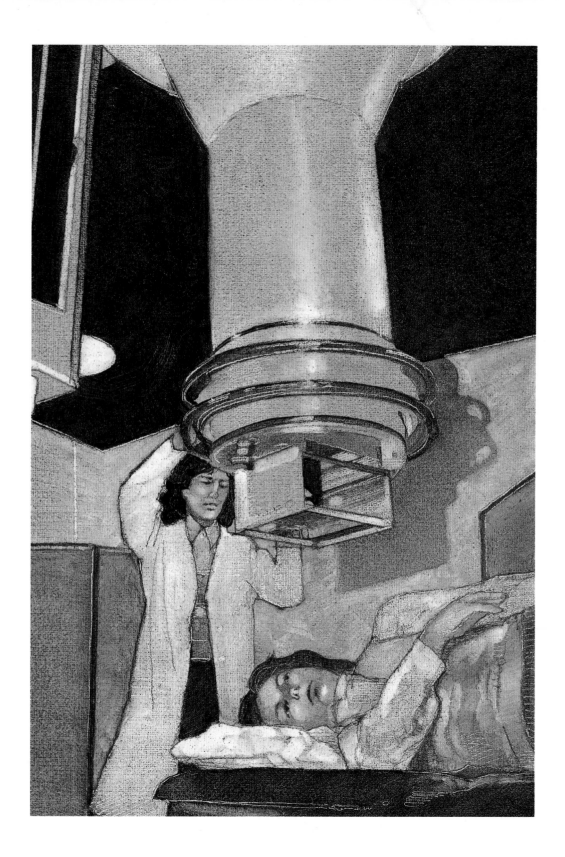

New equipment is being invented all the time. Computers have been combined with X-ray machines to create CAT (computerized axial tomography) scans, which show cross sections or slices of the human body and even of ancient dinosaur skulls.

Soon a powerful X-ray microscope called the Advanced Light Source will be completed. Because it will study living tissue rather than slides from dead specimens, scientists will learn more about how cells in our bodies work. Its beams will also be used to study chemical reactions such as combustion, or burning; the research may someday help reduce pollution.

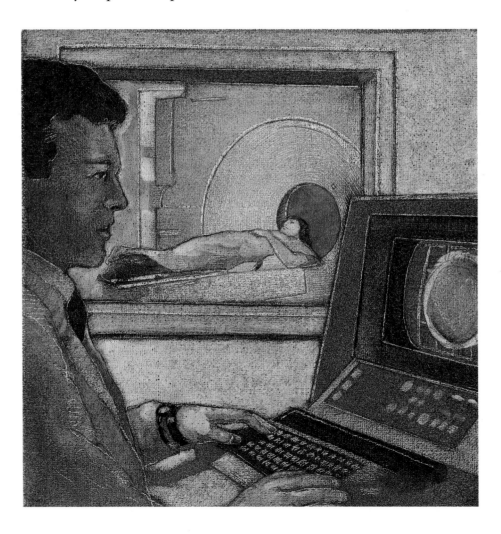

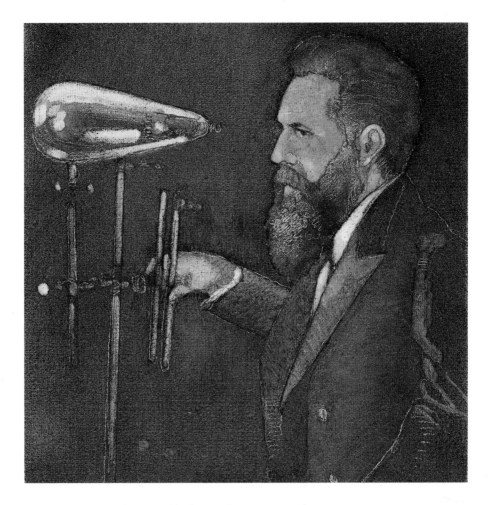

Some say that Wilhelm's discovery of X rays was just an accident. Yet Wilhelm had spent many years working in his laboratory, painstakingly conducting one experiment after another. That November night in 1895 was no different from any other night. He had set up the glass vacuum tube, sent electricity through it, and noticed something unusual. Another scientist might have missed the mysterious green glow or thought it unimportant. Wilhelm did not.

He noticed the glow and knew he had to investigate it. After weeks of repeating his experiments Wilhelm shared his results with fellow scientists. For Wilhelm Röntgen solving research problems was more important than winning awards or getting rich.

AUTHOR'S NOTE

Once Röntgen announced his discovery of X rays, other scientists around the world quickly duplicated his results.

Here in the United States, Thomas Edison began making X rays on a large screen and took out a patent on his methods.

The physicist Michael Pupin claimed he made the first X ray two weeks after he heard about Röntgen's discovery.

Nikola Tesla, who had been experimenting with "visible and invisible" rays, sent Röntgen shadowgraphs he had made even before Röntgen's announcement. Tesla's laboratory burned down and he was unable to continue his research on the rays, but later he invented many useful devices.

Other scientists tried to explain what the rays were. By 1897 Joseph Thomson in England described them as electromagnetic radiations. Some years later German researchers Peter Paul Ewald and Max von Laue came to the same conclusion, saying the rays were similar to light rays but with greater energy.

No discovery is made in isolation. Röntgen benefited from all the research carried on prior to his work. Physicists who came after him added their knowledge step by step. In studying X rays they were all leading to an eventual understanding of the atom and how to harness its energy.

IMPORTANT DATES

March 27, 1845	Wilhelm Conrad Röntgen is born in Lennep, Germany
May 23, 1848	The Röntgen family moves to Apeldoorn, Holland
August 6, 1868	Wilhelm receives his diploma of mechanical engineering, Zurich, Switzerland
June 22, 1869	Wilhelm receives his Ph.D., Zurich
January 19, 1872	Wilhelm and Bertha Ludwig are married
April 1, 1872	Wilhelm begins teaching at the University of Strassburg, Germany
October 1, 1888	Wilhelm becomes professor of physics at the University of Würzburg, Germany
November 8, 1895	Wilhelm discovers new rays
December 10, 1901	Wilhelm is awarded Nobel Prize in physics, Stockholm, Sweden
October 31, 1919	Bertha dies
February 10, 1923	Wilhelm dies

BIBLIOGRAPHY

Caufield, Catherine. *Multiple Exposures: Chronicles of the Radiation Age*. New York: Harper and Row, 1989.

Chang, Kenneth. "High Hopes for Super UC Microscope." *San Francisco Chronicle,* 17 July 1991.

Comroe, Julius H., Jr. *Retrospectroscope: Insights into Medical Discovery*. Menlo Park, Calif.: Von Gehr Press, 1977.

Gardner, Robert. *A Collection of Machines*. New York: Doubleday, 1980.

Ghent, Percy. *Röntgen: A Brief Biography*. Toronto: Hunter-Rose, 1929.

Glasser, Otto. *W. C. Röntgen and the Early History of the Röntgen Rays*. Springfield, Ill.: Charles C. Thomas Publishers, 1934.

———. *Dr. W. C. Röntgen*. Springfield, Ill.: Charles C. Thomas Publishers, 1958.

Macaulay, David. *The Way Things Work*. Boston: Houghton Mifflin, 1988.

Palmquist, Peter E. *Elizabeth Fleischmann: Pioneer X-Ray Photographer*. Berkeley: Judah L. Magnes Museum, 1990.

Roberts, Royston M. *Serendipity: Accidental Discoveries in Science*. New York: Wiley, 1989.

Streller, Ernst, ed. *Wilhelm Conrad Röntgen 1845–1923*. Bonn–Bad Godesberg: Inter Nationes, 1973.

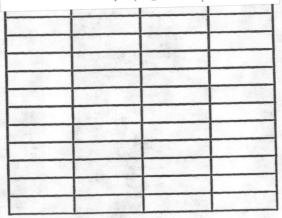